PROMPT ME TO PROMPT YOU

ASA RAY HENSON

First Printing: <2019>

ISBN 978-0-359-17365-5

For any and all contact purposes, please use the following email and mailing address

AsaRayWrites@Gmail.com

Asa Ray Henson
P.O. Box 81
Royston, GA 30662

Hello all and welcome,

I hope you're finding this book out of boredom rather than stressing over attempting to write. However, regardless of what brought you here, I'm stoked to find you between my pages! I hope the tasks written for you here are fun, short, simple, and they bring you inspiration in many ways. May they allow you to grow as a writer, and to even laugh over some of the things you've written and will be writing! I've left about ten extra pages in the back for any notes, muse, or extra space you may need when writing these prompts. You'll find 101 tasks, and I hope that you'll share some of your responses to them along the way! Please, enjoy this goofy little shape of words and ideas.

And, if necessary, always feel welcome to contact me to ask questions, share, or simply be curious with this book.

Find me on Instagram at AsaRayWrites or email me at AsaRayWrites@gmail.com

I'll always do my best to answer, and I will very much show my gratitude.

I hope you find joy beneath the tip of your pen.

(In other words - welcome, to a place of creativity. A space to wipe away the dirt and grim, pick up the key and unlock the door from your writer's block. This is a place of freedom. A space you can speak your mind without any judgement. So, let your words scatter across these pages freely, and please, write what you feel. What you think. What you want to believe. Find yourself alongside your inspiration here. Lastly, thank you for picking up this book and choosing to use the prompts that follow to be a placeholder in the time that is so valuable to you. I hope these ideas help you grow in your writing adventures.)

Happy writing!

Asa Ray Henson

Describe going to a meeting filled with complete strangers

_____

_____

_____

_____

_____

_____

_____

_____

_____

_____

_____

_____

_____

_____

_____

_____

_____

_____

_____

_____

_____

_____

Write about stopping to smell the flowers, describe what you smell

Describe your favorite color without naming the color

You've found a button in an old home you're moving into, what's the story behind it?

_____

_____

_____

_____

_____

_____

_____

_____

_____

_____

_____

_____

_____

_____

_____

_____

_____

_____

_____

_____

_____

_____

_____

_____

Describe going on a date that involves clay

Write about your dream job

As a kid, you've stolen something small from a gas station. Write about either getting caught or not getting caught – what happens? What's the ultimate outcome, and what do you take away from the situation?

_____

_____

_____

_____

_____

_____

_____

_____

_____

_____

_____

_____

_____

_____

_____

_____

_____

_____

_____

_____

_____

_____

_____

Describe buying your dream house

_____

_____

_____

_____

_____

_____

_____

_____

_____

_____

_____

_____

_____

_____

_____

_____

_____

_____

_____

_____

_____

_____

_____

Write five positive things about somebody that frustrates you

_____

_____

_____

_____

_____

_____

_____

_____

_____

_____

_____

_____

_____

_____

_____

_____

_____

_____

_____

_____

_____

_____

Write a letter to your future self

Describe your favorite sin from the seven deadly sins

Write about living inside of your all-time favorite book. Do you take place of the main character? Do you become best friends with the 'star' of the book?

_____
_____
_____
_____
_____
_____
_____
_____
_____
_____
_____
_____
_____
_____
_____
_____
_____
_____
_____

Talk about going without one of your five senses

Describe your favorite superhero – real person or not, who do you consider a superhero?

_____

_____

_____

_____

_____

_____

_____

_____

_____

_____

_____

_____

_____

_____

_____

_____

_____

_____

_____

_____

_____

Write about being thirsty without using the word thirst or parched.

Describe seeing a lighthouse for the first time. What do you notice about it?

_____

_____

_____

_____

_____

_____

_____

_____

_____

_____

_____

_____

_____

_____

_____

_____

_____

_____

_____

_____

_____

Write about seeing life through the eyes of somebody else.

Describe coping with a situation (romantic, an injury, a friendship – whatever your mind creates).

Describe waking in a foreign country, you don't speak the native language. What do you do for the day? Where do you go? What do you eat?

_____

_____

_____

_____

_____

_____

_____

_____

_____

_____

_____

_____

_____

_____

_____

_____

_____

_____

_____

_____

_____

_____

_____

_____

You're lost on an unknown island with no communication to the outside world, what wildlife is around you?

_____

_____

_____

_____

_____

_____

_____

_____

_____

_____

_____

_____

_____

_____

_____

_____

_____

_____

_____

_____

_____

_____

Describe walking through a town that's been destroyed

Describe seeing something nobody would believe you saw if you told them about it.

Write about having a superpower

Describe having a best friend that's a ghost.

_____

_____

_____

_____

_____

_____

_____

_____

_____

_____

_____

_____

_____

_____

_____

_____

_____

_____

_____

_____

_____

Write about a lightning storm that knocks the power out all across town

Describe being in charge of your country for one day

_____

_____

_____

_____

_____

_____

_____

_____

_____

_____

_____

_____

_____

_____

_____

_____

_____

_____

_____

_____

_____

_____

_____

_____

_____

_____

"The ship is sinking, what do we do???"

_____
_____
_____
_____
_____
_____
_____
_____
_____
_____
_____
_____
_____
_____
_____
_____
_____
_____
_____
_____
_____
_____
_____
_____
_____

Describe seeing something nobody would believe you saw if you told them about it.

_____

_____

_____

_____

_____

_____

_____

_____

_____

_____

_____

_____

_____

_____

_____

_____

_____

_____

_____

_____

_____

_____

_____

Write about a missed opportunity..

Write about an old romance.

Write about seeing somebody and trying to get their number or get them to go on a first date with you.

_____

_____

_____

_____

_____

_____

_____

_____

_____

_____

_____

_____

_____

_____

_____

_____

_____

_____

_____

_____

_____

_____

Describe drinking coffee in a rain forest.

_____

_____

_____

_____

_____

_____

_____

_____

_____

_____

_____

_____

_____

_____

_____

_____

_____

_____

_____

_____

_____

_____

Describe taking care of somebody sick.

_____

_____

_____

_____

_____

_____

_____

_____

_____

_____

_____

_____

_____

_____

_____

_____

_____

_____

_____

_____

_____

_____

_____

Write about eating a meal with somebody dead

Describe your pet peeve.

Describe something you're afraid of.

Write about a wild adventure you want to take.

_____

_____

_____

_____

_____

_____

_____

_____

_____

_____

_____

_____

_____

_____

_____

_____

_____

_____

_____

_____

_____

_____

_____

_____

Write about skydiving.

Describe getting arrested for a crime you didn't commit

_____

_____

_____

_____

_____

_____

_____

_____

_____

_____

_____

_____

_____

_____

_____

_____

_____

_____

_____

_____

_____

_____

Write about your favorite tv show as if you were writing the next episode.

_____

_____

_____

_____

_____

_____

_____

_____

_____

_____

_____

_____

_____

_____

_____

_____

_____

_____

_____

_____

_____

Write about breaking things off with somebody.

Describe a silence that seems loud

You wake up in the body of somebody else, what do you do with the new person you are?

_____

_____

_____

_____

_____

_____

_____

_____

_____

_____

_____

_____

_____

_____

_____

_____

_____

_____

_____

_____

_____

_____

_____

_____

_____

_____

Write about touring with your favorite band

When have you had to go against the current of something, what did you do/wish you did?

_____

_____

_____

_____

_____

_____

_____

_____

_____

_____

_____

_____

_____

_____

_____

_____

_____

_____

_____

_____

_____

_____

You can create one new law, what is it?

Write out an adventure you want to take. How much will it cost? Where will you go? What should you see? What will you pack? Will you go alone?

_____

_____

_____

_____

_____

_____

_____

_____

_____

_____

_____

_____

_____

_____

_____

_____

_____

_____

_____

_____

_____

_____

It's raining out and you're stuck inside all day, what do you do?

_____

_____

_____

_____

_____

_____

_____

_____

_____

_____

_____

_____

_____

_____

_____

_____

_____

_____

_____

_____

_____

_____

Describe decorating your first home

Describe living the day in a life of a cop

Describe adopting a child

Write out the goals you want to accomplish this year

_____

_____

_____

_____

_____

_____

_____

_____

_____

_____

_____

_____

_____

_____

_____

_____

_____

_____

_____

_____

_____

_____

Write about traveling the world and trying every coffee you can, what would your favorite flavor be

_____

_____

_____

_____

_____

_____

_____

_____

_____

_____

_____

_____

_____

_____

_____

_____

_____

_____

_____

_____

_____

_____

Describe living the life of a double agent spy.

Write about a rainy day

Describe cooking your favorite meal

Write a list of things that make you happy, laugh, feel safe and content

_____

_____

_____

_____

_____

_____

_____

_____

_____

_____

_____

_____

_____

_____

_____

_____

_____

_____

_____

_____

_____

_____

_____

_____

"Dare to be naïve.."

Describe decorating first home

Write about cooking breakfast with a loved one

Describe going to a concert

Write about working in a coal mine

Learn to write ten phrases of kindness in another language (or multiple languages)

_____

_____

_____

_____

_____

_____

_____

_____

_____

_____

_____

_____

_____

_____

_____

_____

_____

_____

_____

_____

_____

_____

_____

Describe being caught in quicksand

Write some mid-year resolutions/goals

Write a personal letter to somebody

Make a list of pick up lines that boost your confidence

Describe experiencing a natural disaster

Describe discovering an unknown island

Write about swimming with sharks

Write about having your own cooking/reality show

Describe something that makes you sad, then something that makes you happy

_____

_____

_____

_____

_____

_____

_____

_____

_____

_____

_____

_____

_____

_____

_____

_____

_____

_____

_____

_____

_____

_____

If you started your own company, what would it be?

Write about your childhood

Describe sneaking into a party

Write about being an architect

Write about life as if you were a computer

Write about getting an invisible tattoo

Describe uncovering a huge story as a journalist

Write about making amends with somebody

_____

_____

_____

_____

_____

_____

_____

_____

_____

_____

_____

_____

_____

_____

_____

_____

_____

_____

_____

_____

_____

_____

Write a letter to a pen pal

Describe being unable to use one of your five senses for a day

Write a letter of encouragement to somebody

Write a letter of kindness to a homeless person

Attempt a conversation with an inanimate object, then write about it

_____

_____

_____

_____

_____

_____

_____

_____

_____

_____

_____

_____

_____

_____

_____

_____

_____

_____

_____

_____

_____

Write about a rainy day

Describe your favorite drink without naming it

_____

_____

_____

_____

_____

_____

_____

_____

_____

_____

_____

_____

_____

_____

_____

_____

_____

_____

_____

_____

_____

_____

_____

Write about a transformation you've made this year

Talk about something that's inspired you

_____

_____

_____

_____

_____

_____

_____

_____

_____

_____

_____

_____

_____

_____

_____

_____

_____

_____

_____

_____

_____

_____

Write as if you were a pen being used by another writer

Describe leading an orientation for something

Write about your favorite season of the year

Describe going a day without your phone and how you feel

_____
_____
_____
_____
_____
_____
_____
_____
_____
_____
_____
_____
_____
_____
_____
_____
_____
_____
_____
_____
_____
_____
_____
_____

Write about a time you gave something important to you to somebody else

_____

_____

_____

_____

_____

_____

_____

_____

_____

_____

_____

_____

_____

_____

_____

_____

_____

_____

_____

_____

_____

_____

Write a short analysis on the first movie or book that comes to mind

Create a list of metaphors for fireworks

Explain laughter without using the world laugh

_____

_____

_____

_____

_____

_____

_____

_____

_____

_____

_____

_____

_____

_____

_____

_____

_____

_____

_____

_____

_____

Describe the feeling of buying something you've always wanted

_____

_____

_____

_____

_____

_____

_____

_____

_____

_____

_____

_____

_____

_____

_____

_____

_____

_____

_____

_____

_____

Write a letter to yourself